8-05

Dr. Byong Su Kim

Dear Chris,

Best wishes to you as you continue to build your career at the interface of science + business. The selection you chose for your life's work is important, for very few new medications have been developed outside the world of "finance". Good luck to you in your career + personal life — you have a lot the be optimistic about! With best personal wishes

Ray

SIMPLE THOUGHTS

FOR COMPLEX LIVES™

Open Leaf Press
San Diego, CA

For permission to reproduce selections from this
book, please contact:
Open Leaf Press, Attention: Simple Thoughts for
Complex Lives, 8650 Genesee, P.O. Box 927667,
San Diego, CA 92122 or email:
OpenLeafPress@san.rr.com

To order copies of this book, or for more
information, please contact the publisher at the
above addresses, or visit our website at:
www.SimpleThoughts-ComplexLives.com

ISBN # 1-59196-977-8

Classification: poetry, personal growth,
self-reflection, inspirational, motivational

Simple Thoughts for Complex Lives is available in
both hard cover and soft cover.

Printed in the United States of America by
InstantPublisher.com; First Printing, 2005

Published by Open Leaf Press, San Diego, CA

SIMPLE THOUGHTS
FOR COMPLEX LIVES™
(reflections on life, relationships and self)

r.t.bartus

PREFACE

Simple Thoughts for Complex Lives is a collection of poems, poetic essays and observations that deals with the many complexities in our lives, while focusing on the rewards and challenges of personal growth. It is organized into three major sections, each of which reflects one of the more important elements in all our lives:

Part 1: "The Long Journey", or our personal and unique journey through life,

Part 2: "Interconnections", or the relationships we form with others that enrich this journey,

Part 3: "The Looking Glass", or the insight we gain through introspection and self reflection that enables personal growth, thus giving purpose to the journey.

TABLE OF CONTENTS

Part One:

The Long Journey

OUR LIVES

Each of us must travel
our own journey,
stretched out over
a continuum of time—
where the decisions we make,
the experiences we gain,
and the character we show
collectively define who we are...
who we have grown to become...
and for those brief moments
when we get it absolutely right...
all that we were meant to be.

The Long Journey

Reflections

Simple Thoughts for Complex Lives

SUCCESS

One of the more noble challenges of
**   achieving success**
is allowing yourself to grow
**   into something better**
without losing intimate contact
**   or respect**
for the parts of you that are your past.

Simple Thoughts for Complex Lives

FAILURE

**Failure
is simply the act of learning
that another path**

**must be the one that leads
to success.**

Simple Thoughts for Complex Lives

LIVING

Living reflects a process
of continual reinvention,
fueled by a never-ending stream
of new perspectives
and learning experiences.

When that process
is allowed to end,
so, too, does living end--
inadvertently replaced
by another process...
known as dying.

Simple Thoughts for Complex Lives

LIFE'S JOURNEY

If life is indeed a journey,
then poetry must be the
map that reveals
all its topographic possibilities...

while science is the compass
that keeps us from getting lost.

Simple Thoughts for Complex Lives

STARING INTO THE
DEPTHS OF DEPRESSION

Feel the pain and sorrow...
will it ever disappear?
From torn and twisted feelings
of hope, doubt, angst and fear.

Grand plans dissolve to sadness-
cursed by gods we never knew,
while naive dreams become old memories
with no chance of coming true.

Simple Thoughts for Complex Lives

Time is life's
most precious resource...

Use it wisely
and anything can be accomplished.

Waste it too long
and we're left to complain
about the poor hand that fate dealt us

as our most cherished dreams
slip away.

Simple Thoughts for Complex Lives

LIFE LINES WITHIN THE MIND

Some dreams are so perfect...
so precious,
that even though they may come true
for only a fleeting moment--
and never truly seem fulfilled,
they create memories that last a lifetime.

ON THE CONTRADICTIONS
OF FREEWAY DRIVING

Though created by humans
exclusively for humans,
rush-hour, freeway driving
is completely inhuman.

It is mindless--
in that it requires no imagination
or higher intellect;
yet at the same time,
is deeply mind-occupying--
in that any mental lapse can be fatal.

Thus, it holds hostage
our minds and human intellect
inside a dull, inhuman prison--
a suffocating prison
built solely on the bricks
of technology gone bad.

Simple Thoughts for Complex Lives

TRUTH AND
THE SCIENTIFIC METHOD

Truth is the ultimate beauty...
and time its greatest ally.

Yet, within the flow
of human experience,
pseudo-charm of ancient superstitions
and stubborn resistance
of arrogant thinking
constantly conspire to conceal truth
behind biased eyes and closed minds.

Truth's greatest hope, therefore,
lies within the power
of the scientific method
which provides the means to
sift through ideas- good and bad-
while refining abstract concepts
until, inevitably, the truth reveals itself.

The simple elegance of this arrangement
lies in the fact that, once seen so clearly,
truth rarely permits itself
to lie hidden again.

Simple Thoughts for Complex Lives

Aging....
is God's way of reminding us

of all the things
we had intended to do
    - but didn't

and all those things we
shouldn't have done
    - but did.

Simple Thoughts for Complex Lives

Beware of false expectations...

they not only conspire to disappoint,
but perhaps even more importantly,
blind you to other aspects
that you might otherwise
have enjoyed immensely.

Simple Thoughts for Complex Lives

AVOIDING FAILURE WHILE PLANNING FOR SUCCESS

Success rarely, if ever,
occurs by chance.
Thus, it is essential that we not leave
to chance, the individual elements
required for success.

Proper planning for success
requires that we
not only maintain a clear focus
on the ultimate goal,
but also give careful attention
to executing each important detail
along the way.

By achieving the proper balance
between 'fine details' and 'the big picture',
we help assure the likelihood of success...
and in doing so,
also relegate failure to chance.
For, if failure is now to triumph,
it will require the assistance of
some unplanned or chance event.

Simple Thoughts for Complex Lives

DREAMS

**Dreams really do come true,
but mostly for those who have
the faith to believe they will...
the insight to see what must be done...
and the will to make
each small opportunity
bring the dream one step
closer to reality.**

TIME

That grand healer of all wounds
but silent force beneath all decay.
Designated as life's most precious resource
in the eyes of our elders
and most abundant wasteland
in the lives of our youth.

Arguably the most powerful—
yet least understood force of nature,
time carves graceful canyons
through sturdy stone walls,
while sculpting delicate dreams
from the magic still buried
within our child-minds.

(cont.)

That perpetual catalyst of all change,
time holds hostage the final resolution
to life's most passionate struggles—
struggles that remain temporarily suspended
while time subtly drones its complex rhythm
of gradual transformation:
  Time for reflection... revelation...retreat.
  Time for growing... outgrowing...
    growing weary of.
  Time for living... reliving fond memories...
    outliving the need for.

As time passes, it inevitably weaves
a complex tapestry of continuous change
from the seemingly isolated events
that comprise our lives...
until at some point in time,
the colored patterns within this tapestry
reveal a truth that each of us
must eventually face-
The time has finally come for us
to begin an entirely new journey,
where even time itself will start anew.

Part Two:

Interconnections

PARENTING

Being a parent is the most common --
yet most difficult and complex
of all human experiences.

As parents, we proudly accept responsibility
for those we love the most
but at the same time are humbled by the cold fact
that we must try to guide their development
in a world where we have very little genuine control.

As parents, a primary objective
is to make the path easier for our children
through the success we achieved and
the lessons we learned during our lives;
yet we must constantly be reminded that
our children are not us...
and their lives are not ours.

We share our life's lessons with our children
so that they might avoid our mistakes
and escape some of our pain,
but unwittingly expose them to our own
personal prejudices and frustrations,
thereby corrupting their dreams
and inevitably altering their direction
in ways we never intended.

(cont.)

Because we are parents,
we are sometimes seen as the worse enemy
by the ones for whom we care the most.
Yet, in a heartbeat
they can overwhelm us with intense joy
by confirming their appreciation
through a simple smile or a whisper
from their lips saying 'I love you'
as they fall asleep.

Aside from the sheer joy
that parenting can bring,
the lessons, rewards and strength we gain
prepare us to meet any other challenge
that life might present.
For with each hug at the end of a hard day
we are continuously reminded
that the really serious issues-
the most important problems in life-
revolve around trying to be good parents.
And this insight makes all of life's other problems
seem a bit less important...
and thus more manageable.

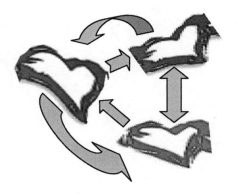

Interconnections

Reflections

CONTRACTS OF THE HEART

When sharing love
or loaning our hearts,
we should always save
the largest portions
for family and for those friends
who we have known the longest...

for in the end, we always learn
that they are the ones
who prove most deserving.

Simple Thoughts for Complex Lives

PROMISES

The value of a promise...

**lies not in the sincerity
with which it was made...**

**but in the determination
with which it is kept.**

Simple Thoughts for Complex Lives

TRUE FRIENDS

**True friends are those
to whom we can reveal
our emotional warts
and intellectual deficiencies,
without looking less attractive.**

Simple Thoughts for Complex Lives

LIFE'S FABRIC

Friendship... Understanding... Trust...

when properly interwoven with Love,

provide the basic fabric of Life.

Simple Thoughts for Complex Lives

LOVE ENDURING

Falling in love can be wonderful
but often far too easy.

For maintaining the initial beauty of love
as time struggles to reshape our worlds
and put space between common bonds...

is the challenge
that helps give love purpose...
... and makes life worthwhile.

Simple Thoughts for Complex Lives

Love and the Burdens
of Growing Old

Growing old presents many burdens
    in varied forms,
but not so the love that is earned
    as one grows old.

For that love, which takes seed
    very early in our lives and
continues to blossom gradually
    throughout one's lifetime
represents the purest form
    of human exchange...

wherein the giver often receives
    far more than the recipient.

Simple Thoughts for Complex Lives

Caring is the greatest gift
that one can give to another;

Understanding is the greatest love.

Simple Thoughts for Complex Lives

CHARM AND INTEGRITY

Charm and integrity--
two very different,
yet parallel, attributes.

Charm
can move mountains
through sheer persuasion
when cooperation is essential.

Integrity
can serve as a mountain of principle,
to distinguish right from wrong
when opposing forces blur that line.

While all of us,
have some of each...
few of us
have an abundance of either.

Those who have
an abundance of both...
walk as gods
among mere mortals.

Simple Thoughts for Complex Lives

ON COMMUNICATION

To communicate complex
thoughts or emotions
one must first achieve
intimacy with them.

Therefore, first let the idea
enter your heart-
so that you might feel it; then

let it enter your soul-
so that you might understand it;
and finally,

let it enter your mind-
so that now you might be able
to express it.

Simple Thoughts for Complex Lives

ON THE ACCUMULATION
OF WEALTH

When one considers wealth and
our life's effort to accumulate it,
it is clear that those people who
seem most genuinely happy,
are those who have learned
that money's greatest value
comes from its ability
to allow love to be shared...
and joy to be spread...
in ways that would otherwise
be entirely impossible.

Simple Thoughts for Complex Lives

PRINCIPLES OF TRUST

**Strong relationships breed
pledges of trust and
promises of confidentiality.**

**But honoring these pledges
after a relationship has deteriorated,
raises a fundamental question
that challenges human nature:**

**Should the principle be abandoned,
simply because the relationship has?**

Interconnections

Intimate Reflections

LOST IN DREAMS

I'm sure they were there—
the nay-sayers who warned you
that I was not worth the effort;
that in the end,
you would surely be disappointed...
but you looked to me and I whispered:
"Come with me, girl; get lost in my dreams".

Later, we vowed to spend our lives together.
'Mere children', people snickered;
'far too young and immature—
certain to ruin each other's lives'...
but I promised you
we'd be O.K. and pleaded:
"Come with me, girl; get lost in my dreams".

(cont.)

Gradually, we built a life together
while enduring lonely moves...
humbling sacrifices... daunting risks.
Friends and family questioned
many of our decisions,
but you trusted me as I beckoned you:
"Come with me, girl; get lost in my dreams".

Today we approach
the autumn of our lives...
together still--
our lives more than half consumed--
our children, grown adults.
With so much to appreciate and yet—
so much life left to share,
I now look at you and thank God.
For without you, girl,
I would be lost...
wandering aimlessly in an empty sea
of unfulfilled dreams.

Simple Thoughts for Complex Lives

LOVE, LIFE AND YOU

An almost casual glance;
   a simple, child-like kiss...
A humble beginning eons ago,
   until that seed and the love
that bloomed from it have become
   the foundation of my life.

The years rush by,
   yet the days last forever.
So many happy moments
   that each almost goes unnoticed; yet-
their memories fill a lifetime.
Such is my marriage to you
   and the love we've shared.

After years on this journey,
   it's become increasingly clear to me
that without your love,
   I would be but a fraction of myself, for
Love, Life and You...
   have become one and the same for me.

Simple Thoughts for Complex Lives

LOVE AND ROSES

Love forsaken
    is like a trampled rose...

The bruised and broken pieces
    hardly reflect the pain endured--
    or beauty lost.

But they do reveal the stark reality
    that this one
    will never bloom again.

WE TWO

I remember you
when you were but a child...
and I've accompanied you
as you have become
a beautifully sophisticated
and worldly woman.

I've lived with you
through many changes-
including great struggles
and grand times -
and through each chapter in our lives,
it seems as though
there has always been
just you... and me.

(cont.)

We've grown to know
each other so well
that I often know your thoughts...
even when you're far away.

I think of you...
even when I'm sleeping.

I remember you...
even when I seem
to be thinking of nothing.

And you sneak into my consciousness...
even when my mind seems filled
with thoughts of everything else.

Through our years together,
ever so delicately,
you have crept inside my soul, until today,
you are within me... and I within you.
Each of us is a part of the other-
as inseparable as Siamese twins
bound at the head, the heart and the soul.
We two, are one....forever.

Simple Thoughts for Complex Lives

SOLACE IN YOU

I learned long ago
that I am far from perfect
and I have accepted
that I have only so much
time or love to give.

But I find solace
in knowing that we will
love each other forever,
and in recognizing that my
greatest satisfaction comes
from the simple times
we share and the love
we give to each other.

Simple Thoughts for Complex Lives

EVOLVING THOUGHTS
ALONG THE SAD GOODBYE
(Kristin's Revelation)

Summer's gone... Winter's near...
cold, gray skies paint over blue.
Birds chase south in desperate flight
crying when, again, will I see you?

How deep is your love for me?
Is it too aggravating?
Is it burning? Is it dead?
Or lying dormant... waiting?

The reality of what we had
becomes more clear with time.
It was far less love... or you,
but mere illusions in my mind.

Simple Thoughts for Complex Lives

Within You

From the time of my teen age years,
whenever I searched
for anything of lasting value,
I looked to you
and together we found it.

Time passed on- our lives entwined–
and, gradually, I learned that
much of what brought me
true happiness resided within you–
and all I had to do
was look to you to find it.

Today, as we gradually grow old together
I realize that the things
most important to me
are all part of you...
and the deeper I search,
the more I find... within you.

Simple Thoughts for Complex Lives

Our Love

Love happens....
  and I thank God everyday
  it happened to us.

Time changes all things...
  and I continue to feel blessed
  that our love has persisted
  through all our changes.

Few things last a lifetime...
  and with each passing day
  I am even more grateful to you
  for helping to make our love
  the exception.

Simple Thoughts for Complex Lives

Silent Reflections of a Weary Traveler

Happiness is just a fragile state of mind...
and sadness, passing pain
within the heart.

But loneliness is like a cloud
whose shadow comes and goes--
as I miss you... and want you...
and patiently hunger for you
when we're apart.

Simple Thoughts for Complex Lives

A MARRIAGE VOW

To you I pledge my love
    as long as I shall live.

I give my heart to you
    as long as I can give.

My lips shall call your name
    as long as they breathe life.

These sacred vows I swear to keep,
    for you-- my love-- my wife.

WHEN LOVE DIES
(Ode to my sister)

Somewhere deep inside-
in a place that few have seen-
It's there; sometimes quietly nagging,
sometimes consuming-
but, always filling your soul
with a dull, burning pain-
knowledge that he's out there,
but no longer part of your life.

In another place
where few others have ever been-
fading memories become inadequate.
Where once bold emotions raged
as though they'd last forever,
and promises of eternal love flourished,
now only faint images remain...
a shrinking space in your heart
that's still reserved for only him.

(cont.)

Gradually, that space grows smaller
as the distance grows greater-
distance no longer measured in miles...
but in time.

Occasionally a fleeting memory
revives suppressed feelings--
feelings that plead to be free-
to grow- to be part of you again...

But always the pain endures,
reminding you of the absolute futility:
What happens in your heart
matters not at all...
for the love you knew in his,
has already died.

Part Three:

The Looking Glass

Prolog: The Looking Glass

A BOY AND A HILL

Though now removed by many miles
and even more years- it must still be there-
a small hill on the edge of the woods
with steep-sloping sides covered
with lush green clover.
A warm breeze flows gently along the
clover top spreading the fragrance
of flowers and wild grass
while bright colored butterflies
gently brush the air and yellow honey bees
excite the area, flying to and fro.

Often, as the rest of the world seemed
to frantically rush by
I would lie down on the soft clover blanket,
staring into the huge sky
while the sun sent rays of warmth
throughout my body.
As the cotton-white clouds rolled
across the vast horizons of the sky,
visions of valiant knights
and errant pirates raced through my mind.

Hour after hour I would enjoy
the wonderment of my make-believe
world in the clouds.
Over time, the clouds would slowly begin
to drift away as the air gradually cooled,
ultimately leaving only an empty,
immense, deep purple sky.

(cont.)

It seemed like I spent a lifetime
of summers on that hill...
until one day, as I was descending its slopes,
and looked back over my shoulder,
a nostalgic lump filled my throat
as a tear invaded my eye.
Somehow I realized that this would be
the last day that I would visit the hill,
for soon I would be a man and the magic
of visiting here would no longer be.

Many years have long passed
since I spent my summers visiting that hill.
And only now, in the autumn of my life,
do I finally begin to appreciate
how blind I had become.
The magic of that hill had never
abandoned me, after all;
rather, I simply chose to ignore it.
For now I understand that
throughout all of our lives
hills such as that have always existed.

To find the magic in our hill,
we each merely need to look...
And never forget why it is
we're looking.

The Looking Glass

Reflections

Simple Thoughts for Complex Lives

HONESTY

**Because our perceptions
are strongly colored
by what we already believe to be true,
it is impossible to be completely honest
with the world,
without first being completely honest
with yourself.**

DECEPTIONS PRECLUDED

The facade has been dismantled,
the masquerade unveiled;
Transparent, pseudo-charm exposed-
the gods of truth prevail.

The facade is stripped away at last;
our vision cleared to see.
The devils of deceit denied,
our destiny set free.

Simple Thoughts for Complex Lives

RUNNING FROM ONESELF

The greatest limitation to running away
from any of life's problems
is that we have no alternative
but to take ourselves along...
no matter where we try to run.

And for that reason, alone,
nothing ever is truly solved
until we first commit to
confronting ourselves.

Simple Thoughts for Complex Lives

Adulation must be one of the more
ironic human feelings...

The more one actively pursues it...
the more elusive it remains.

The more easily it is achieved
the less value it possesses.

Simple Thoughts for Complex Lives

Problem Solving

One of the greatest obstacles
we each face when searching for
solutions to problems
is the false assumptions
we invariably and unwittingly make.

One of the greatest impediments
we face when trying to execute solutions
is our own self-delusion.

Identifying and minimizing
these two factors, therefore,
provides the simplest means possible
for increasing our chance of success.

Simple Thoughts for Complex Lives

DECISIONS

Sometimes an ounce of insecurity
is worth a pound of confidence...

A touch of uncertainty
worth a ton of courage.

Simple Thoughts for Complex Lives

**Confidence is being able to see
so far into the future...
you no longer feel
the need to look.**

ALZHEIMER'S PLEA

Cloud my senses... steal my strength,
I surrender these to age and time.
But spare my human dignity
and take my life before my mind.

Simple Thoughts for Complex Lives

ON DISCIPLINE
AND THE PURSUIT OF GOALS

We say "practice makes perfect"...
yet, "no one is perfect".

Clearly, few of us seem
guilty of too much practice.

Simple Thoughts for Complex Lives

SELF EVALUATION

Each time we evaluate our actions
primarily by the outcome that ensues
and not with regard to the
principles applied-
or the quality of judgment exercised,
we deprive ourselves of the opportunity
for personal growth
that may otherwise have been possible.

Simple Thoughts for Complex Lives

ANOTHER YEAR

Another year... another wrinkle,
another year... more gray hair.
Another year for me to ponder--
this key to life- I'm now aware.

Another year to fix the damage—
correct the faults within my past,
for as lives flow we all must wonder
if this year <u>may</u> ...
just be our last.

SILENT REFLECTIONS

A dull, heavy pain
burns deep within my chest-
a constant reminder that he is gone
and I will never see him again.
It feels as though some chunk of my being
has been ripped out and trampled over,
never to be repaired.

The apparent suddenness
with which this has happened
has left me ill-prepared.
I find emotions swelling up inside me,
even when my mind seems to be far removed
from thoughts of him.
Yet, at some level I must be thinking of him.
Or, is this merely a reflection
of the huge void
his passing has created?

Occasionally, I seem to sense his presence,
as if he is trying to communicate with me.
He assures me that things really are alright
and I should not worry about him;
rather, I should make certain my Mother is O.K.;
I should love my siblings at all cost;
I should strive to lead a good life.

(cont.)

When I find solace in these moments,
is it because he really is communicating
with me from some higher cosmic level,
or is this merely my imagination
trying to soften the intense loss I feel
until I am ready to deal with
it more rationally?

I struggle to understand
that which is not understandable
until eventually I tell myself that,
for the moment at least,
it really does not matter.
He is gone.
I will never see my father's smile
nor hear his laugh again.
Death is indeed final.

Alas, one thought keeps recurring
as I find myself too choked to talk:
Each time we said "Hello"
and especially
the last time we said "Goodbye",
I wish I had hugged him longer.

Epilog:
Simple Thoughts for Complex Lives

METAMORPHOSIS OF AN EAGLE
(a tribute to Ron Kovic and the triumph of personal growth)

METAMORPHOSIS OF AN EAGLE
(A tribute to Ron Kovic and the triumph of personal growth)

War is a game -
where the mundane issues
of childhood life
are momentarily pushed aside as we
soar through open fields
at breakneck speed
or cultivate youthful versions
of passion and suspense
by cautiously crawling under brush
in search of imaginary enemies
not quite our equal.

If war is a game then
the parade is its celebration.
Where the sounds of spirited trumpets
swell my chest with pride
and the cadence of snare drums
drives my heart into a hard,
synchronized beat
as they awaken the patriotic
spirit hibernating
in child and adult, alike.

(cont.)

Parades are war's living showcase
where the real soldiers —
from the real wars
march together - arm in arm —
brother with brother
as huge crowds look
on with admiration
and the prettiest women in town
ride the newest convertibles,
blowing kisses of adulation
to my heroes.

(cont.)

War is more than a game...
war is a reflection of life -
with all its challenges and opportunities.
Where you can stretch your wings
and soar to heights otherwise unreachable.
And with keen eyes, clear mind,
quick body and strong will
I know I possess all the tools required...
and war is my vehicle.

War is my best shot to gain their respect -
to confirm my own self-respect -
to prove to others what
I already know about myself.
To forever rise above
the last vestiges and petty constraints
of a childhood
that continues to linger too long
within the memories of family
and neighbors around me.
To free myself from the adolescent bondages
of sibling rivalries,
meaningless responsibilities and
arbitrary parental codes of behavior.

(cont.)

Yes, war provides the opportunity
to establish one's rightful position
in the overall scheme of things -
among family and friends -
among neighbors and society.

To prove without a doubt that I am worthy -
worthy to stand along side
the other real men of our country
and graciously accept the hero-worship
bestowed on us by all the rest.

(cont.)

War is no game -
for in games there are winners.
Rather, war is dirty business
and its filth accumulates progressively.
Over time it obscures one's vision
and stains one's conscience
until the thin line
separating right from wrong
and good versus evil
becomes increasingly difficult to sight.

War forces you to view things differently.
Once you have learned to peer through
the self-doubt, disillusionment and fear -
though the trumpets may still blow -
their sound is now muffled.
Your once crystal-clear goals have faded into
naive, ambivalent notions...
Your once razor-sharp visionary purpose
is forever lost.

War is insane. War is suffering.
Where often the bravest men
are the ones most scared -
where each man must search
for his own way of handling the fear -
and his own private way of crying.
Where even the children
get pulled into the abyss of madness
and even though they are the only ones
who still seem able to smile,
their pain is no less real...
their wounds no less tragic...
their death no less final.

(cont.)

Where the elderly -
who have toiled throughout long hard lives
to reach their final position
of peace and serenity -
who patiently prepare themselves
to receive answers
to life's most Eternal questions -
must instead languish -
trapped inside this man-made hell
for which they have no role-
able only to stare out through fixed,
expressionless eyes
in quiet disbelief.

War hardens you
to the pain and misery
it thrusts upon you
but it does little to prepare you
for the void created
by its deceptions and delusions.
How can something
that once caused such fire
to burn deep within my soul
now leave me absolutely numb?

(cont.)

War may indeed be a game,
but not for those who fight its battles
and fall victim to its cruelty.
Rather, war is played and controlled
by nameless, far away people
who construct and manipulate
ambiguous rules
in pursuit of selfish, hidden agendas

War moguls - who prey upon
your sense of pride
and fundamental loyalties -
asking from you the ultimate sacrifices,
while offering in return
only those intangibles
you already possess.

Though you risk losing your life -
or more - they quickly abandon you
when you no longer
serve their purpose –
sentencing you
to an isolated state of exile
within your own bankrupt soul.
Abandoning you into a desolate world
where all that exists is a barren horizon
accented only by the gloom
cast from your own shadow.

(cont.)

In the isolation of your thoughts
you are forced to recognize that
though they trained you how
to fight their war,
they never prepared you
to fight this private war
raging within yourself.
And though they taught you
to hate impassionately,
they never warned you
that you inevitably would end up
hating yourself the most.

Locked in a world
of endless frustration and desperation...
cut off from the hope
of reestablishing genuine relationships
with family members and long time friends...
taunted by memories
which recur in only two forms-
those that haunt and those that tease...
Suspended in a world of utter despair
I struggle to simply survive, until at last
my vision begins to clear...
The longer I sit trapped
on this motionless bag of half-dead flesh
the more I begin to realize
that my only means to regain any freedom...
my only hope for achieving inner peace...
is through communicating to others
these solemn truths that
I have learned myself.
Then... and only then...
can I finally lay this war to rest.

Postscript
About This Book

The poems and passages that comprise this book were written and compiled by the author throughout his adult life. He also conceived and developed the book's title, concept, organization, design and cover. The illustrations were personally selected or created to complement and visually enhance the written text. Together, they are intended to provoke contemplation and facilitate reflection, while also entertaining and helping to personally enrich the reader.

The author dedicates this book to his mother, Katherine, whose early belief and unfailing encouragement were invaluable, and to his deceased father, Frank, who taught through love and example, the values of discipline, sacrifice and responsibility.

The author gratefully acknowledges his wife, Cheryl, who has been at his side, growing together, forever... or so it seems. Obviously, most of the 'Intimate Reflections' were written for her. Cheryl's support and patience during the completion of this project, as well as her helpful feedback in the selection of certain illustrations and on other aspects of this book, are also greatly appreciated and acknowledged.

ABOUT THE AUTHOR

Though r.t.bartus (Raymond T. Bartus, Ph.D.) has enjoyed writing poetry since he was 12 years old, he has devoted his life's career to science. He received a doctoral degree in the neurosciences at the age of 25 and has since worked primarily in the pharmaceutical and biotech industries as a scientist and executive, both conducting basic research, as well as contributing to the research and development of several new products for human diseases.

Dr. Bartus is recognized as one of the originators of the 'Cholinergic Hypothesis of Alzheimer's disease', a concept that led to the first four drugs approved by the FDA for Alzheimer's disease. He has written and published over 200 scientific articles as well as edited several scientific books. He founded and for 10 years served as Editor-in-Chief for Neurobiology of Aging, the premier journal in its field; he remains a Section Editor for that journal, today. He has been honored by the Institute of Scientific Information (ISI) as a "Highly Cited Researcher", placing him among the top 99.5% of all scientists, based on the impact of his research on that of other scientists.

Dr. Bartus holds adjunct appointments at Tufts University Medical School and New York University Medical School and has served on select panels for the U.S. Congress' OTA, the Alzheimer's Association, the FDA, the Secretary of U.S. Department of Health and Human Services, and several institutes within the NIH, in fields as diverse as aging, drug abuse and cancer. He is listed in *Who's Who in America, Who's Who in the World, Who's Who in Science* and *Who's Who in HealthCare,* among others.

In addition to science and writing, the author enjoys time with close friends and family, fine wine, music, history, golf, sports and outdoor activities. He has two adult children and lives with his wife, Cheryl, in San Diego. They met and started dating in high school and have been married for over 30 years. Dr. Bartus is currently Sr. Vice President and Chief Operating Officer of Ceregene, a biotech company focused on treatments for Alzheimer's, Parkinson's, ALS and similar neurodegenerative diseases.

ORDERING INFORMATION

To order additional copies of this book, please:

➢ write the publisher at: Open Leaf Press, Attn: Simple Thoughts for Complex Lives, 8650 Genesee, P.O. Box 927667, San Diego, CA 92122

➢ email: OpenLeafPress@san.rr.com

➢ contact your favorite bookstore, referring to ISBN # 1-59196-977-8 to identify this book.

For additional information on this book, please email or write the publisher or visit our web site at: www.SimpleThoughts-ComplexLives.com

Simple Thoughts for Complex Lives is available in both hard cover (US$19.95, plus postage and tax) and soft cover (US$11.95, plus postage and tax).

OPEN
LEAF